When All Else Fails ...
Try Success

When All Else Fails ...
Try Success

Nick Kasik

iUniverse, Inc.

New York Lincoln Shanghai

When All Else Fails ... Try Success

iUniverse books may be ordered through booksellers or by contacting:

iUniverse
2021 Pine Lake Road, Suite 100
Lincoln, NE 68512
www.iuniverse.com
1-800-Authors (1-800-288-4677)

Because of the dynamic nature of the Internet, any Web addresses or links contained in this book may have changed since publication and may no longer be valid.

The views expressed in this work are solely those of the author and do not necessarily reflect the views of the publisher, and the publisher hereby disclaims any responsibility for them.

ISBN: 978-0-595-47389-2 (pbk)
ISBN: 978-0-595-91667-2 (ebk)

Printed in the United States of America

Contents

Introduction

With everything we do, we all strive to be successful both in our business life, and our personal lives, but unfortunately we are not taught how to be successful. At home we were all taught by our parents to follow the rules, get a good job, and do our best. In school, we were all given the fundamental tools to function in the working world. But somehow, it never dawned on any one to actually teach us how to be successful. Today everyone tells their children that it is good enough just to try. Failure has somehow become acceptable, as long as you tried.

So as adults trying to improve ourselves, we all buy books like this hoping to get some insight to the business world, and hoping to pick up the one little secret that solves all our problems. But it never fails, we never seem to come upon this little secret, because it is no secret at all. We just simply need to change the way we think. We need to stop trying and start thinking and acting like a successful person in order to become a successful person. You see, it's not what we do or what we know, it's how we think that makes the difference.

I would love to take all the credit for this simple concept, but unfortunately I can not. I must share the credit for this concept with one of the most respected business men that I have ever had the pleasure to work with. Mr. Tom Sanders, is a giant in the mechanical contracting and construction industry, who preached this concept to everyone that would listen and many more who would not listen, for years and years.

The sad part is that I never really got it. That is, until it started to sink in and I really started to change the way I approach issues, and how I think. Once I changed my thought process it became more and more clear to me, and suddenly I noticed that I was enjoying more and more success.

I was a young construction project manager in my mid 20s, working for Mr. Sanders' company, and every quarter we would sit down and discuss the financials of our projects. We would talk about the wins and losses, and how we were managing the project. He would always tell us, "When All Else Fails … Try Success". Well I never really took it serious, because it sounded a bit rhetorical and didn't really seem like a concept I could actively apply. Well guess what? Now I realize just how profound the concept he was trying to share with me was, and it was not long for me to realize that success works every time you try it. You just have to figure out how to apply it.

Now, I know, the first time you hear this, your mind immediately asks the question, "Okay, so what do I do?" Well, I can tell you right now, that if you asked that question in your mind, then you still don't get the concept. It's not about what you do, it's about what you are. You don't do successful, you are successful. Stop thinking about ways to be successful, and just start being successful.

It's kind of like the statement: "You can lead a horse to water but you can't manage him drink." We are taught to manage people, when we need to be leading them to do what they want to do anyway. Then we simply convince them do what they want to do, but to do it for us as managers and leaders. You must strive to get as many people as you can doing what you need them to do, because they want to do it, and you will then be on the road to becoming a success. We all tend to over think it all by trying too hard to be a good manager, good businessman, good whatever, and not just doing what we need to do to be successful, letting the success take care of itself.

In this book you will find some rather simple concepts that will help you along the way of the path to changing you from a thinker to a doer, and from a manager to a leader, and from purposeful to successful. You will find that this is not the usual long winded business self-help book that you might find at the airport or your local bookstore, but this is a concise simple concept that doesn't require a lot of instruction. It starts with having a clear vision of what success is, and includes many hints and pointers that can help you every day.

In reading this book, it is important to remember that it is not a magic answer to your problems, nor is it a text book or a roadmap to success. It is up to you to implement what you read and learn in this book everyday. You need not memorize the information, or get lost in the details of the chapters. Instead, you need to remember to absorb the concepts. As you read this book you either will get it or you won't. If you do get it, the light will come on and it will just make sense. If you finish the book and you don't feel that the light went on, re-read it over and over until the light comes on. Then refer back to the book for ideas you can apply to specific situations. The book will work for you, if you take it serious and are willing to change the way you think.

1

Charisma

For a moment, step outside your body and take an honest look at yourself. Would you hang out with you? Be honest. If you don't see yourself as an interesting person that would be fun, and cool to hang out with, then probably no one else does either. But you still have friends coworkers that want to be around you right? Or do you? Take a hard look at yourself, and your friends to make sure that your "friends" are not just looking for something, and playing the game because they feel you can provide an avenue to success for them.

If you are honest with yourself, and you don't see yourself as that person, then you will seriously need to consider reinventing yourself. If you are that person, then you need to continue to improve this image and your personal skills.

This is where it all starts. If you can't get this chapter mastered, then you need not worry about any of the rest of the book. It will all become simple and make perfect sense, because everything in this book builds upon the information in this chapter. The level of success you will enjoy from here on out, will completely hinge upon how well you can apply the information in this chapter. I would suggest reading this chapter and then re-reading it, before you go on to the following chapters. It is that important.

However, you must also remember that this is the most difficult chapter in the book. All the other chapters build around implementing specific concepts and ideas that you can apply. This chapter requires that you take an honest look at yourself, and be willing to see your flaws for what they are, and that you be willing to totally start over and re-invent yourself.

The word charisma refers to a rare trait found in certain human personalities usually including charm and a 'magnetic' quality of personality and/or appearance along with powerful persuasiveness. Though very difficult or even impossible to define accurately, charisma is a personality trait that includes the ability to lead, charm, persuade, inspire, and/or influence people. It refers especially to a quality in certain people who easily draw the attention and admiration of others. It is not only the way you act or carry yourself, but also your appearance. First impressions are everything. Do not underestimate the power and importance of the first impression. You only get one shot at it. You want to leave people with two impressions:

First, you want people to genuinely like you and your personality. You want them to remember you and want to be around you. You want to create a level of professional respect and confidence that they will want to work with you in the future. But also, you want them to want to be your friend. You want to exude a casual friendliness that makes people want to hang out or go have a beer with you.

Second, you want people to remember you by sight. You want to be recognizable. If I had a dollar for every time someone told me I looked familiar to them, I would be giving these books away. Those of you that are attractive have a natural advantage. The rest of us have to find a way to separate ourselves. Use your traits to your advantage. I have a thick, full head of hair, but I shave it every morning, because it is part of my trademark look. You have to go out on a limb and find what works for you. But become recognizable.

Developing your charisma is one of the most important things that you can do on your journey to becoming successful. It makes sense because people do business with people, not businesses. It is a proven fact that attractive people are more successful, so do not underestimate the importance of your appearance. If you are not attractive, find a way to stand out and be memorable.

You need to have marketing skills. I know, your first thought is that you are not in marketing and sales, so you do not need these skills. But the fact of the matter is that all truly successful people, regardless of their business, are great sales and marketing people. Notice though, that the real key is that they may not market their product or service as much as they market themselves. Go sell yourself to everyone everyday. You never know who you might meet, or end up sitting next to on a plane, so always be making that sale.

Here is a fine example. My wife and I went away for a short weekend get-away to a nice little resort in Mesquite, Nevada. We were in line to get registered for an entertainment venue, and my wife, who is the most upbeat, bubbly, personality you would ever meet, struck up a friendly conversation with the lady behind the counter processing our transaction. Well, by the end of this 5 minute transaction, the lady ended up cutting us a check to comp our hotel room in the resort, simply because she liked us and we made her day just a little bit better.

Looking at it on a larger scale, look at what Donald Trump does. We all think of him as a smart and successful businessman because he has power, money and real estate all over the world. Well in order to buy his first property to renovate and sell, he had to sell himself, and his ideas, to someone that would loan him the money. He had to market himself rather than the project, because the project was what it was, and would be the same project no matter who did it. The difference he had to sell was that the involvement of Donald Trump would make the difference at the end of the day. Was the project any better because Donald Trump was involved? Who knows? At this point who cares? But the fact remains that he sold himself, and the rest is history, as they say.

The fact of the matter is that when you market yourself at every level, as the difference between success and failure, everyone will unwittingly work to ensure that you are successful, because everyone likes associated with a winner. It is your job to have the confidence to inspire everyone you meet along the way to blindly trust your judgment, because they believe you are smarter and better connected than they are.

By nature people are followers. They want to be lead into the sunset by the hero on the white horse. Well as long as you tell them from day one that you are that hero, and that you can lead them into that sunset if they just get on board with you, they will do what needs to be done, and make you look like a hero.

You must ooze confidence, but not to the point of elevating yourself too far above everyone else. You must be confident, but approachable and real. You have to be a bit of a chameleon to connect with the people in the trenches, but also impress executives and investors. You need to be able to make people question themselves and think that you are smarter and more cunning than they are. You must convince them that you will defeat them before they even engage with you.

Intimidation is the most powerful tool you can develop. Now understand that this is also the hardest tool to develop, and many very successful people never master the ability to intimidate. But for those who can, it can be a huge advantage. If you can master the ability to convince others that you are not only smarter, but you will stop at nothing to get your way, and you will not hesitate to crush anyone in your way, you will have developed a huge advantage for yourself.

However, I would only suggest working on this trait, if you are confident that you have all the others under your belt. Remember that if you attempt to intimidate someone, and they call you on it, you will be forced to follow through, or back down. And most likely at this point in your development, you have nothing more than a bluff.

Below are the Ten Commandments of Charisma:

1. FIRST IMPRESSION!

There is nothing more important than a great first impression. People will size you up in less than 10 seconds so be sure to make eye contact, speak first while giving a firm handshake and, make sure you are focused and engaged on the other person during the introduction, and remember their name. It makes a huge difference in developing trust.

2. RESPECT YOURSELF

This goes back to first impressions. Once you have cultivated your style, build upon it. Whatever your style, whether you dress in Italian suits and drive BMWs, or dress in black denim and ride a Harley Davidson, stick to it, and be neat & clean. It doesn't matter if you spend $50.00 on a haircut or shave your head for free, just be neat, clean and consistent. As long as you indicate that your style is who you are on purpose, and that you respect yourself enough to spend a little on yourself, people will respect that. Just remember to keep your style within reason for those who you are going to be around. Don't go to the bank in search of a loan dressed like a punk rocker, unless you're in a punk rock band.

3. RESPECT OTHERS

Even if you disagree with the other person/people, respect them anyway. They will be far more likely to respect your opinion and consider another viewpoint when you don't put them on the defense. It is completely acceptable to disagree with someone as long as you don't attack them or force them to defend themselves.

4. MAKE EYE CONTACT

Look me in the eye when you talk to me. Eye contact establishes domination. Have you ever had a stare down with a dog? If you win, you own that dog. People are no different. If you establish eye contact when you are serious and relax eye contact when you are not, it helps people read you how you want to be read. If you master this technique you will dictate what read people take on you. They will think they are reading you, but all they are really getting is what you are giving them.

5. ASK QUESTIONS

Most people just want to talk about themselves anyway so show a genuine interest in them, their family, and their interests, but don't get too personal, and you will find that they will tend to like you more. It also helps you to learn about what's important to them before you meet them, if possible. It will help prepare you provide a product/service that they may need.

6. BE ATTENTIVE

Make sure you are constantly focused on the person that you are talking to. Nothing else matters for the time that you are talking to this person. Stop whatever you are doing and focus on them. When you are distracted or looking past them, it shows that you are not interested in what they have to say. Always be gracious.

7. NO JUDGMENTS

Gossip and public judgments about other people's characters are always a no-no. You will always make people wonder if you will talk about them behind their backs. Always have class. Always act as though you pay no attention to these things. It will differentiate you as a leader.

8. BE NICE

Have you ever seen the movie Roadhouse? There is a scene in the movie where the bouncers are being taught to "Be nice". If there is a problem, take care of it, but be nice. If there is a disagreement, defend your side, but be nice. Be forceful, but be nice. Be right, but be nice. Be confident, but be nice. Be serious, but be nice. If you don't know what I'm talking about, you need to rent the movie, because there is a ton of value in this message.

9. WARMTH

Be warm and accepting of other people. Simply showing a genuine concern and engaging with the other person will always convey warmth. Some people are naturally more aloof or perceived as cold. If that is you, this is something that you will have to make a conscious effort to change ... but the results will be immediately worth it.

10. BE HUMBLE

It always makes people uncomfortable when you constantly brag about your successes. When you focus on other people's successes, people tend to be more appreciative. When you're always humble, your successes tend to be magnified anyway—without you having to say a word about it.

Now re-read this chapter ... It's that important!

2

How to Lead Rather Than Manage People

To manage is to lead, and to lead is to set the example. If you expect others to follow, you need to set the pace as it pertains to work ethics, do what it takes to get the job done, and do it as a professional. Every day you can view an example of how not to lead by watching the news on TV and see how our politically appointed representatives bend the rules and in some cases, simply lie under oath. As a result, politicians are not the most highly regarded professionals.

The antonym for leadership is follower. Some are born followers, no matter what they do. They just don't apply the skills required to be a leader. However, leaders are not just born either, they are developed. One still has to apply the skills required to be a leader.

On the road to developing yourself as a leader, follow the following guidelines for success:

1. **Honesty:** Once I was told by someone that they didn't agree with my position on a particular topic, but they knew I wasn't lying to them. I took this as a complement.

2. **Communication:** You should only close your office door when you have people in your office for a conference call. The background noise of the office that caries through the phone can be quite distracting. Otherwise, you want to be available to communicate with others.

3. **A positive attitude:** You cant lead if you're complaining. The only time you can voice a complaint, is if you follow it up with a suggestion for improvement.

4. **Dress for success:** Dress the part. If you are a service manager, dress as a manager of technicians, not as a banker. If you are an engineer, dress as a professional and not as a laborer. It is as important not to over dress as it is to not under dress.

5. **Teach to replace:** Hire people that are smarter than you. Don't be afraid to have highly intelligent people working for you, you will learn from their feedback. Also remember that you can not be promoted until you train your replacement.

6. **Mentoring:** The better the personnel, the better the product. Train by sharing you experiences both good and bad with your people. Help others to set goals, and contribute to the team. A leader can not do it all by themselves.

7. **Time Management:** This is the cornerstone of getting it all done and getting it all done on time and on budget. This skill will carry over to your personal life and increase the quality of your life at home.

8. **Delegation:** Delegation. It's worth saying again because you can't do it all yourself. If you achieve the above things trusting your people and giving up portions of your workload, then meeting your responsibilities becomes easier, and you appear to others to be more successful.

Results are the stuff that leaders are made of. If they're not getting results, they won't be leaders for long. Results come in countless forms and functions. But one thing they all share: they are material consequences of actions. You can't see strength, you can't hear it, you can't smell it, you can't taste it, you can't feel it; however, if you ignore the non-material that the strength encompasses, you'll be short on your leadership.

Have you ever worked for someone that you did not respect? I really sucks working for managers that you can not respect. Either they hide behind their power, their education or their position, everyone knows that they couldn't do the job that they are asking you to do. Worse yet, is the manager that preaches ethics but their ethics are completely suspect.

Remember that leadership is by example. If you are not ethical, then it will reflect on you and the company, tainting the reputation of everyone in the company. As a manager, especially a top level manager, you need to remember that ethics start with you. Don't be tempted to profit on the backs of your employees. Profit with your employees. If your salary or bonus is way more than that of the producers that you have working for you, then you are on the road to destruction. Slavery is over, so don't underpay the people that pay your salary. Don't become self-involved and begin thinking that you are actually worth more than your top performers, because you are not. If you believe this, the next thing you know you will be sitting across the table competing against them instead of with them.

To be successful we must work with and for others toward a common goal of achieving some result. To be able to achieve our goals we must be able to relate to others effectively. Here is a list of ideas will help you be viewed as a leader rather than a manager.

- Catch people doing things right and then let them know that they are doing things right.

- Use feedback to stay informed about what other people are doing in your area of responsibility and authority.

- Have regular, focused meetings regarding the projects that you are responsible for.

- Provide adequate instructions. Time is lost if things are not done correctly.

- Train others to do jobs. You cannot do them all, nor can others do them if they have not been trained.

- Expect others to succeed. It becomes a self-fulfilling prophecy when you believe others are loyal, dedicated and doing a good job.

- Help others see how they will benefit from doing a job. This is when they truly become motivated.

- Do not avoid talking to a poor performer. It hurts them, the organization and yourself if the situation is not dealt with.

- Do not over control others. It is frustrating for them and time consuming for you.

- Focus on results, not on activities or personalities.

- Reward people for the results that they produce.

- Manage by walking around. See what people are doing and listen to what they have to say.

- Consider sharing distasteful tasks to reduce resentment and hard feelings.

- Ask, "Will you please do this for me" instead of telling someone just to do it.

- Eliminate private secretaries in favor of shared secretaries in order to make it easier to even out the work load.

- If you give employees a basic employee handbook, you will not be interrupted with their questions.

- Pay attention to small details, the big ones are obvious and get taken care of.

- Stay open in your thinking. Be open to all new ideas. Do this and you will not be setting up barriers that do not exist.

- Avoid asking others to do trivial personal items for you.

- Say thank you to those with whom you associate.

- A warm smile and strong handshake break barriers.

- Smile. It helps you feel better and is contagious. The whole organization shudders when the boss is frowning. Likewise it smiles when the boss does.

- Always give people the benefit of the doubt. They may not be the cause of a problem. The cause may be beyond their control.

- Admit it when you do not know the answer to a question posed by a staff member. Then challenge the staff person to research and decide what the best answer is. It will help this person grow.

- When you were away and some of your people did an exceptional job, call them at home in the evening when you find out and personally thank them for what they did instead of waiting until the next time you see them.

- If you know that a person will respond angrily to a particular comment, avoid bringing it up. It is nonproductive and bad for the relationship. In other words, "never kick a skunk."

- Make quality an obsession, especially on smaller items.

- Send thank you notes and memos.

- Provide workers with open, direct, and immediate feedback on their actual performance as compared to expected performance and they tend to correct their own deficiencies.

- Practice naive listening. Don't talk, just let people explain why they are doing the types of things that they are doing. You will learn many things.

- Manage by exception. When things are going well, leave them alone. When a problem occurs, then help.

- Never seek to place blame. Always focus on the problem.

- Never ignore a concern of one of your people. While it may seem trivial to you, to the other person it is a problem that will continue to destroy their train of thought.

- Make it a personal rule and a challenge to respond to someone within 24 hours of hearing their request.

- Keep memos on bulletin boards to a minimum. People will spend less time standing there reading.

- When you are going to make a change that affects others, get them involved before making the actual change. This increases commitment to make the change work after it is implemented.

- Put key ideas on small posters to hang around the office.

- When the environment and your sincerity permit, give the person a hug or a touch.

- Employees are the only organization resource that can, with training, appreciate in value. All other resources depreciate.

- People want to be involved in something important. Give them a whole project or a significant piece of the project to work on.

- Have salary tied into performance appraisal and accomplishing of objectives.

- Be persistent and follow up.

- Give employees an opportunity to speak their opinions and suggestions without fear of ridicule or reprisal.

- When you appreciate what someone has done, let them know and put it in writing. This can then be added to their personnel file.

- Have an opinion survey done to determine how people view the organization. That way you can catch any problems while they are still small.

- Encourage periods of uninterrupted activity such as a daily quiet hour in your department or work group.

- When asking someone to do something, let them know what is in it for them and the organization. Do not focus just on what is in it for the organization and yourself.

- Keep things "light" and have fun rather than being too serious. Seriousness blocks productivity.

- In order to fly with the eagles you must "think lightly."

- Work with each person to create standard operating procedures for their specific job. It will eliminate repetitious questions.

- Let people know why they are doing something. It then becomes more meaningful when they recognize their part in a greater vision.

- Provide soft, lively background music not slow and not rock.

- To get a disorganized coffee drinking crew started off more efficiently, begin each day with a 5 to 10 minute meeting just at starting time. They will be focused, set in the right direction and can get right to work.

- Practice the golden rule in business: Do unto others the way you would have them do unto you. Fairness will then be in your business.

- Practice the platinum rule in interpersonal relationships. It is "Do unto others, the way they want to be done unto." They will be more apt to stay comfortable when interacting with us when we are able to do things their preferred way.

- Consider sharing ideas and responsibility with others rather than just getting someone to do it for you or just doing it yourself.

- Inspire others to new levels of achievement by using positive encouraging feedback and ideas.

- Set the stage for cooperation from others by:1) Introducing the idea; 2) Continual stimulation by talking about it; and 3) get others to make an investment by having them participate in the planning.

- If you are unable to reach agreement or get a commitment from another person in a meeting, agree to disagree, but summarize your understanding in a confirming memo.

- Giving people recognition generates energy within them. They will then direct that energy toward increased productivity.

- Tap the potential of those working for you by giving them opportunities to think things through for themselves instead of just telling them how to do something.

- The boss is the strongest model the employees have. Be a positive model as people are watching to see how you behave. They will reflect this in their own behavior. Lead by example.

- Be a member of the 4 F club with others. Be seen as Fair, Firm, Friendly and having Foresight.

- Do not help others unless they need and ask for help.

- Encourage your people to come up with new ideas and ways to do things. Give them credit and recognition for the idea.

- If a new idea won't work, at least praise the effort of the person so they will come up with future ideas.

- Get others to commit to deadlines by asking, "When can you have that for me?"

- Nail down commitment by asking, "Do I have your word that you will have that for me then?"

- Encourage others to develop their plan of action and give you a detailed explanation.

- Encourage individuals to compete against themselves to achieve more. Let it be a personal challenge to become better as an individual-not competing with others but self.

- Check the ratio of positive comments to negative comments that you make to your people. Purposely make more positive comments.

- Demand accountability.

- Do things for others. They will be more willing to do things for you.

- Consider using time off as a reward for getting things done ahead of time.

- Set up an orientation training program for all new employees. It will help them learn their way around as well as teach them where things are kept and why.

- Stay informed of subordinates' needs and interests. Projects can be more effectively designed and rotated when you are well informed.

- If individuals needs some encouragement in taking action, ask them, "What if ..." questions to help them see what choices of action are available.

- Let people know that you know they can do it.

- Ask questions creatively so the action to be taken is suggested by the person who is to take it.

- Set up incentives that reward desired performance.

- Ask others for their estimate of how long it will take to do a project. When possible, agree and hold them accountable for that goal.

- Take on someone else's routine so they can do what you need done without interruption.

- Just as with family members, break large chores up into small, fun activities and enjoy doing them with team members.

- Before an employee leaves on vacation agree on a "must do" list of activities to be completed.

- Do not be quick to judge others. Learn to listen carefully before coming to conclusions.

- Once a month meet with each staff member to catch any problems or concerns the person may have as soon as possible before they become a crisis.

- Be the kind of a person that others want to help out and work for.

- Be flexible and do whatever it takes to get the job done. Remember it is results that count, not activities.

- Generally speaking, getting something done perfectly is usually not as important as getting it done. Perfection has a high cost and it may not be worth it.

- When giving or receiving information, don't hurry. Take the time needed to truly understand. It prevents future problems and misunderstandings.

- Whenever you are having an important discussion with a person, before parting, set a specific follow-up date and time and write it in your calendar.

- Never criticize an employee in front of others. Have all discussions of a corrective nature in private.

- Hire people with specific skills and interests that match what the organization needs to have accomplished. The better the match, the better the productivity and the more motivated the person.

- Treat people as people-not things.

- Flaring in anger will drive others away. If not physically at least mentally,

- Keep a "warm fuzzy" file for each person a place to keep track of the things you have already complimented them for, and want to compliment them for.

- Have regular performance review and goal setting sessions with each of your employees at least every three months.

- Have regular "development discussions" with each of your people in which you discuss only how the individual may grow personally and how you and the organization may be able to support them in doing this.

- Low morale in workers may be an indication of the boss only talking about negative things or what's wrong. Be sure to balance negative comments with more frequent positive comments.

- Let your people know you are there to help them not to harass them.

- Telling people what you plan to do, and when, can be a catalyst for getting objections and input which you might not otherwise receive.

- Form an action team to address people's problems right away rather than letting things drag out and perhaps get worse.

- Instead of saying to another, "What can I do for you?" ask them "What can you do for me on this project?"

- Do not hold back from discussing the need to improve performance with one of your people.

- Don't just ask someone who is busy to get things done for you; look for the busy person who is getting results. This is a doer, not simply a busy wheel spinner.

- Believe in the good of people.

- Do not be a "baby sitter" of others, constantly taking care of them and telling them what to do. Challenge them and help them learn to think and do things for themselves.

- Consider an incentive plan to reward productivity gains.

- Don't do what you can get someone else to do by simply asking.

- Clearly communicate who you want to do what, by when and at what cost. Then identify who needs to know about it and when they are to be informed.

- For people you relate to regularly, keep a list of things you need to talk to the person about. Then when you meet with or call them, you can review all the items that have accumulated on your list.

- Recognize you are not the only one who can do a job right. Trust others to do things for you.

- Organize, deputize, supervise.

- Meditate for one minute before starting a new subject or project.

- Don't worry about who gets the credit for completing a project. Focus on the task to be accomplished and do it.

- When credit is given to you for completion of a project, be sure to give it to all who were involved. This will nurture the relationships and provide motivation to support you in the future.

- Be sincerely interested in the people working for and with you.

- Help others recognize their own importance.

- Keep a list of birthdays, marriage and work anniversaries and other special dates. Provide recognition to your people on each of these dates. Mark your calendar prior to the actual date so you have time to prepare for it.

3

Delegation

Delegating work, responsibility, and authority is difficult in a company because it means letting others make decisions which involve spending the owner-manager's money. At a minimum, you should delegate enough authority to get the work done, to allow assistants to take initiative, and to keep the operation moving in your absence.

This chapter discusses controlling those who carry responsibility and authority and coaching them in self-improvement. It emphasizes the importance of allowing competent assistants to perform in their own style rather than insisting that things be done exactly as the owner-manager would personally do them.

"Let others take care of the details." That, in a few words, is the meaning of delegating work and responsibility.

In theory, the same principles for getting work done through other people apply whether you have 25 employees and one top assistant or 150 to 200 employees and several managers. Yet, putting the principles into practice is often difficult.

Delegation is perhaps the hardest job managers have to learn. Some never do. They insist on handling many details and work themselves into early graves. Others pay lip service to the idea but actually run a one-man shop. They give their assistants many responsibilities but little or no authority.

Authority is the fuel that makes the machine go when you delegate work and responsibility. It poses a question: To what extent do you allow another person to make decisions which involve spending your company's money? Yet, if an owner-manager is to run a successful company, you must delegate authority properly. How much authority is proper depends on your situation. At a minimum, you should delegate enough authority: To get the work done, To allow key employees to take initiative, and To keep things going in your absence.

Delegation of responsibility does not mean that you say to your assistants, "Here, you run the shop." The people to whom you delegate responsibility and authority must be competent in the technical areas for which you hold them accountable. However, technical competence is not enough.

In addition, the person who fills a key management spot in the organization must either be a manager or be capable of becoming one. A manager's chief job is to plan, direct, and coordinate the work of others.

A manager should possess the three "It's"—initiative, interest, and imagination. The manager of a department must have enough self-drive to start and keep things moving. A manager should not have to be told, for example, to make sure that employees start work on time. Personality traits must be considered. A key manager should be strong-willed enough to overcome opposition when necessary and should also have enough ego to want to "look good" but not so much that it antagonizes other employees. Competent people want to know for what they are being held responsible.

When you manage through others, it is essential that you keep control. You do it by holding a subordinate responsible for his or her actions and checking the results of those actions. In controlling your assistants, try to strike a balance. You should not get into a key manager's operation so closely that you stifle him or her should you be so far removed that you lose control of things.

You need feedback to keep yourself informed. Reports provide a way to get the right kind of feedback at the right time. They can be daily, weekly, or monthly, depending on how soon you need the information. Each department head can report his or her progress, or the lack of it, in the unit of production that is appropriate for his or her activity; for example, items packed in the shipping room, sales per territory, hours of work per employee.

Periodic staff meetings are another way to get feedback. At these meetings, department heads can comment on their activities, accomplishments, and problems.

For the owner-manager, delegation does not end with good control. It involves coaching as well, because management ability is not acquired automatically. You have to teach it.

Just as important, you have to keep your managers informed just as you would be if you were doing their jobs. Part of your job is to see that they get the facts they need for making their decisions.

You should be certain that you convey your thinking when you coach your assistants. Sometimes words can be inconsistent with your thoughts. Ask questions to make sure the listener understands your meanings. In other words, delegation can only be effective when you have good communications.

And above all, listen. Many owner-managers get so involved in what they are saying or are going to say next, that they do not listen to the other person. In coaching a person so he or she can improve, it is important to tell why you give the instruction. When a person knows the reason, he or she is better able to supervise.

Sometimes you find yourself involved in many operational details even though you do everything that is necessary for delegating responsibility. In spite of defining authority, delegating to competent persons, spelling out the delegation, keeping control, and coaching, you are still burdened with detailed work. Why? Usually, you have failed to do one vital things. You have refused to stand back and let the wheels turn.

If you are to make delegation work, you must allow your managers freedom to do things their way. You and the company are in trouble if you try to measure your assistants by whether or not they do a particular task exactly as you would do it. They should be judged by their results—not their methods.

No two persons react exactly the same in every situation. Be prepared to see some action taken differently from the way in which you would do it even though your policies are well defined. Of course, if an assistant strays too far from policy, you need to bring him or her back into line. You cannot afford second-guessing.

You should also keep in mind that when an owner-manager second-guesses assistants, you risk destroying their self-confidence. If the assistant does not run his or her department to your satisfaction and if his or her department to your satisfaction and if his or her shortcomings cannot be overcome, then replace that person. But when results prove his or her effectiveness, it is good practice to avoid picking at each move he or she makes.

Good decision making is an essential skill for career success generally, and effective leadership particularly. If you can learn to make timely and well-considered decisions, then you can often lead your team to spectacular and well-deserved success. However, if you make poor decisions, your team risks failure and your time as a leader will, most likely, be brutally short.

Leaders who make correct decisions, without time wasting delays are seen as decisive, courageous, insightful, brilliant, and successful. Leaders who stall, who seem unable to make up their mind, who waffle, who procrastinate, and obsess with the fear of making mistakes are seen as not leaders who can make believers of his or her employees, but someone about to lead the business into a disaster or difficult times at best.

How do your employees see you? Are you the executive or entrepreneur who has a track record of making the wrong decision? Do you have a tough time making up your mind, or are you impulsive? If you are about to cash out the equity in you home and launch a new business or expand your business, the wrong choice can ruin you. Look inward, how do you see your skills?

Are you afraid of making the wrong move? Fear immobilizes. If you are fearful of making a mistake the natural tendency is to put off making a choice-hiding your fear behind the excuse of analysis or thoughtful leadership. Fear can lead to lost opportunities. And your disguised fear of failure will drive your employees nuts, I am sure you know such people they can be maddening.

Yet, there are times when you should put off any action, as what ever you choose is likely to be the wrong choice. If you are over tired, not feeling well, emotionally upset, or feeling impatient when you are not up to snuff-you are prone to error, so wait a day or two until you are your normal self. To put the odds in your favor, you need to be healthy and have clear head; strong emotions will color your decision making not good!

Equally disastrous is acting on impulsive, falsely thinking that great leaders bark commands, make decisions as the commercials show the busy executive briskly walking with his entourage tossing off major decisions as if he or she were ordering lunch.

As a leader your are required to make decisions like it or not. Here is a technique you may find helpful. Do you understand the downside of your decision? What is the worst that can happen if you are wrong? Can you live with it? If not, the gamble may not be worth the risk. Successful stock market traders have a cardinal rule, that they will not risk more than 5 to 10 percent of their capital on any one trade. They know bad trades happen and they know they will make mistakes. They understand that risk management is crucial to their success. So don t be eager to bet your business on a single decision.

The greater the impact, on your business, your lifestyle, your finances, and your future, the more difficult it is to make a decision. Somehow, you must find a balance between the rewards of risk and the probability of success. You must look at the advantages and disadvantages of your choices. It is a valuable tool to help you make such decisions as opening your own business, expanding your operation, investing in a new product, or taking in a partner.

As you struggle with your choices be careful about soliciting opinions if you do so, remember those giving you such advice are looking at your situation with their own frame of reference and emotions. And how you present your possible plans will effect what you hear. Getting opinions from family and friends is not the same a getting a medical second opinion, you don t ask a neighbor if you should have a knee operation. Decisions are part of life, and daily part of being in business. If you hate to choose or live in fear of making a mistake, sharpening your decision skills is just one more hurdle you must over come as you work to become a successful leader.

There are times our decision-making is stalled due to fear of making the wrong decision. Next time you're in that indecisive state of mind, answer these questions and see if it pushes any buttons to move the process forward.

- What is the "best case" desired outcome?

- Will your decision move you toward that outcome?

- What is an "acceptable" outcome?

- What is the worst thing that could possible happen if you make the "wrong" decision? Can you accept this?

- Is your decision reversible?

- Will a wrong decision destroy value, confidence or trust of anyone involved?

- Do you have enough information to make the decision?

- Do you have too much information?

- Who knows more about this subject than you … what are their recommendations?

- Are you the right person to be making this decision?

- Will avoiding making a decision now make the situation better, worse or have no effect?

- Does the decision provide a short term fix or will it solve the problem permanently (long term)?

4

Vision

Think fast! What's your company's mission statement? Can you recite it? Can your employees? Do you even have one? Do you even care? All the business experts will tell you that you must know what this mission is, and you should memorize it because it is what will be the difference in your company.

While it's imperative for every company to be able to properly articulate its mission, because your mission statement is the cornerstone of what your firm stands for. Your mission/vision statement is about your ultimate destination. It's about the fact that your company has a goal and vision. Your mission statement is about how you plan to get to your goal. It should describe your company's unique and enduring reason for being, making it clear why anyone would want to do business with you rather than your rivals.

Done right, a mission statement will guide and inspire your staff, help you decide how to allocate scarce resources and create shared values to turn your company into a competitive force. Unfortunately, too many firms do it wrong.

Most missions fall well short. They may get the wording wrong by failing to say the right things, or worse, by saying the wrong things, such as "our employees are our most important asset." Even if the words are right, they may never be translated into action.

Now, having discussed the importance of a mission statement, as I have said before, and will say again, ultimately it isn't about what you are going to do to implement your mission statement, it is about just knowing what to do to be successful, and not having to try to be successful. In other words, it is a tool. It is not your instruction statement, or your guide to success. The mission statement is a tool that you may use in your successes.

Often there's too much detail in a mission statement. Although there's no absolute rule about length, many good ones run 10 to 20 words. Go too short, and you won't provide enough guidance. Go too long, and you'll saddle yourself with a list of priorities too long to implement effectively. Limiting the word count forces you to decide what truly differentiates your firm for stakeholders.

How often do you refer to your mission statement in staff meetings? Do your managers have to relate their plans and budgets to it? Do you use it as the basis for training, recruitment, promotion, reward and disciplinary programs? Does your management-information system track progress against the mission?

It's well known that you can't manage what you don't measure, and that what gets rewarded gets done. But many companies that claim to be mission-driven don't measure their progress against their mission and fail to reward staff for helping make it a reality.

The true worth of an organization's mission comes from the extent to which it is practiced, not just professed. The payoff from getting it right, from aligning your mission with your firm's resources, is a juggernaut organization that will roll over competitors that have not developed the same degree of focus and commitment.

There is no easy recipe that guarantees a successful vision-in-action. Make it specific. An inspiring statement is great, but people interpret things very differently. The people of your organization need specific examples of what behavior is consistent with the vision of the organization. If you service your customers, what does that sound like when the receptionist answers the phone? What are your customer service reps empowered to do to solve problems? How will you know if you've achieved the best service, and how do the specific departments throughout the company contribute to that result?

By enlisting employees' and customers' perspectives, you're building momentum and support for your vision while gaining valuable insight into the potential strengths and weaknesses of your approach. Set up a forum where employees can easily and freely exchange ideas, a survey, an online conversation, a staff meeting, a column in your company newsletter, a "brown bag" luncheon series, a suggestion box or a graffiti wall. Gain input from customers in similar ways.

See the vision through others' eyes. It can be difficult to share information (or even think you have to) when you come from a completely informed perspective, as is often the case when leaders have been immersed in planning and are impatient, or are pressured by the board of directors, once it's time to implement. Think about how the initiative will change the way employees work. What information or skills do they need to be successful? What do customers experience? Is that consistent with the vision?

Capitalize on what's already working. How do employees get other information? How do partners and customers get information? Are these channels appropriate for your messages? The point is an old one, but it works here: Don't reinvent the wheel if the wheel works fine. Share your messages via avenues that employees and customers already tap for information, and augment your repertoire to fill information gaps.

Make the connection. People are committed to other people or projects based on their own internal motivations, not a dictate from someone else. Relate an employee's tactical accomplishments to the business goals, make associations between employees' actions and the effect on the bottom line, and highlight activities that are consistent with the vision. Connect your "world class service" rhetoric with a customer's experience of being in phone system hell for 40 minutes waiting to get a problem solved, only to be told someone else handles it (and she's on vacation).

Make your vision part of the organizational discourse. Over time, people will understand that it's a direction in which the organization is going, not simply a quick-fix management theory pulled from the latest guru's book (which is, unfortunately, often how it's approached). Take a fresh look at your vision; how can employees help make it a reality? Why not ask?

The most important point I want to make is that a mission statement is very important to an organization. It is a guide to your goal constantly reminding you, your staff and your clients of what you are trying to achieve. However, at the same time it is not your road map. If you have to think about it and put effort into implementing your mission statement, then you are not on the road to true success. You are not trying success, you are implementing the last management guru's ideas that you just read in a book.

5

Time Management

The role of leader can be very stressful! Management studies have suggested that these roles include a very wide mix of activities, most of which cannot always be controlled or even predicted.

New managers and supervisors, especially supervisors, are almost overwhelmed with the demands of the job. They were probably promoted to be in charge of people, mostly because of their success in a previous role that was focused on developing a particular product or service. Suddenly, they're faced with being in charge of people, which is much less predictable and has much less control than the supervisor had before. Consequently, the ability to manage time and stress is absolutely critical to the success of the roles of manager and leader. The two topics of time management and stress management are often addressed together because they are so closely interrelated.

I will start by telling you some myths About Stress and Time Management:

- All stress is bad. No, there's good and bad stress. Good stress is excitement, thrills, etc. The goal is to recognize personal signs of bad stress and deal with them.

- Planning my time just takes more time. Actually, research shows the opposite.

- I get more done in more time when I wisely use caffeine, sugar, alcohol or nicotine. Wrong! Research shows that the body always has to "come down" and when it does, you can't always be very effective then after the boost.

- A time management problem means that there's not enough time to get done what needs to get done. No, a time management problem is not using your time to your fullest advantage, to get done what you want done.

- The busier I am, the better I'm using my time. Look out! You may only be doing what's urgent, and not what's important.

- I feel very harried, busy, so I must have a time management problem. Not necessarily. You should verify that you have a time management problem. This requires knowing what you really want to get done and if it is getting done or not.

- I feel OK, so I must not be stressed. In reality, many adults don't even know when they're really stressed out until their bodies tell them so. They miss the early warning signs from their body, for example, headaches, still backs, twitches, etc.

Major Causes of Workplace Stress

- Not knowing what you want or if you're getting it—poor planning.

- The feeling that there's too much to do. One can have this feeling even if there's hardly anything to do at all.

- Not enjoying your job. This can be caused by lots of things, for example, not knowing what you want, not eating well, etc. However, most people always blame their jobs.

- Conflicting demands on the job.

- Insufficient resources to do the job.

- Not feeling appreciated.

Biggest Time Wasters

- Interruptions. There will always be interruptions. It's how they're handled that wastes time.

- Hopelessness. People "give in", "numb out" and "march through the day".

- Poor delegation skills. This involves not sharing work with others.

Common Symptoms of Poor Stress and Time Management

- Irritability. Fellow workers notice this first.

- Fatigue. How many adults even notice this?

- Difficulty concentrating. You often don't need to just to get through the day!

- Forgetfulness. You can't remember what you did all day, what you ate yesterday.

- Loss of sleep. This affects everything else!

- Physical disorders, for example, headaches, rashes, tics, cramps, etc.

- At worst, withdrawal and depression.

Principles of Good Stress and Time Management

- Learn your signs for being overstressed or having a time management problem. Ask your friends about you. Perhaps they can tell you what they see from you when you're overstressed.

- Most people feel that they are stressed and/or have a time management problem. Verify that you really have a problem. What do you see, hear or feel that leads you to conclude that you have a time or stress problem?

- Don't have the illusion that doing more will make you happier. Is it quantity of time that you want, or quality?

- Stress and time management problems have many causes and usually require more than one technique to fix. You don't need a lot of techniques, usually more than one, but not a lot.

- One of the major benefits of doing time planning is feeling that you're in control.

- Focus on results, not on busyness.

- It's the trying that counts—at least as much as doing the perfect technique.

There are lots of things people can do to cut down on stress. Most people probably even know what they could do. It's not the lack of knowing what to do in order to cut down stress; it is doing what you know you have to do. The following techniques are geared to help you do what you know you have to do.

- Talk to someone. You don't have to fix the problem, just report it.

- Notice if any of the muscles in your body are tense. Just noticing that will often relax the muscle.

- Ask your boss if you're doing OK. This simple question can make a lot of difference and verify wrong impressions.

- Delegate.

- If you take on a technique to manage stress, tell someone else. They can help you be accountable to them and yourself.

- Cut down on caffeine and sweets. Take a walk instead. Tell someone that you're going to do that.

- Use basic techniques of planning, problem solving and decision making.

- Concise guidelines are included in this guidebook. Tell someone that you're going to use these techniques.

- Monitor the number of hours that you work in a week. Tell your boss, family and/or friends how many hours that you are working.

- Write weekly status reports. Include what you've accomplished last week and plan to do next week. Include any current issues or recommendations that you must report to your boss. Give the written status report to your boss on a weekly basis.

- Do something you can feel good about.

There never seems to be enough time in the roles of management and supervision. Therefore, the goal of time management should not be to find more time. The goal is set a reasonable amount of time to spend on these roles and then use that time wisely.

- Start with the simple techniques of stress management above.

- Managing time takes practice. Practice asking yourself this question throughout the day: "Is this what I want or need to be doing right now?" If yes, then keep doing it.

- Find some way to realistically and practically analyze your time. Logging your time for a week in 15-minute intervals is not that hard and does not take up that much time. Do it for a week and review your results.

- Do a "to-do" list for your day. Do it at the end of the previous day. Mark items as "A" and "B" in priority. Set aside two hours right away each day to do the important "A" items and then do the "B" items in the afternoon. Let your answering machine take your calls during your "A" time.

- At the end of your day, spend five minutes cleaning up your space. Use this time, too, to organize your space, including your desktop. That'll give you a clean start for the next day.

- Learn the difference between "Where can I help?" and "Where am I really needed?" Experienced leaders learn that the last question is much more important than the former.

- Learn the difference between "Do I need to do this now?" and "Do I need to do this at all?" Experienced leaders learn how to quickly answer this question when faced with a new task.

- Delegate. Delegation shows up as a frequent suggestion in this guide because it is one of the most important skills for a leader to have. Effective delegation will free up a great deal of time for you.

- If you are CEO in a corporation, then ask your Board for help. They are responsible to supervise you, as a CEO. Although the Board should not be micro-managing you, that is, involved in the day-to-day activities of the corporation, they still might have some ideas to help you with your time management. Remember, too, that good time management comes from good planning, and the Board is responsible to oversee development of major plans. Thus, the Board may be able to help you by doing a better themselves in their responsibilities as planners for the organization.

- Use a "Do Not Disturb" sign! During the early part of the day, when you're attending to your important items (your "A" list), hang this sign on the doorknob outside your door.

- Sort your mail into categories including "read now", "handle now" and "read later". You'll quickly get a knack for sorting through your mail. You'll also notice that much of what you think you need to read later wasn't really all that important anyway.

- Read your mail at the same time each day. That way, you'll likely get to your mail on a regular basis and won't become distracted into any certain piece of mail that ends up taking too much of your time.

- Have a place for everything and put everything in its place. That way, you'll know where to find it when you need it. Another important outcome is that your people will see that you are somewhat organized, rather than out of control.

- Best suggestion for saving time—schedule 10 minutes to do nothing. That time can be used to just sit and clear your mind. You'll end up thinking more clearly, resulting in more time in your day. The best outcome of this practice is that it reminds you that you're not a slave to a clock—and that if you take 10 minutes out of your day, you and your organization won't fall apart.

- Learn good meeting management skills. Meetings can become a terrible waste of time. Guidelines for good meeting management are included later in this section. Manage yourself, not your time.

Many of us claim our days are never wasted. "I'm very organized" we say "I know where I am going and what I'm going to do". If you truly feel that way then you are in the minority. Most people become frustrated with a day that is unproductive. We would all like to get more done in a day

The idea of time management has been in existence for more than 100 years. Unfortunately the term "Time management" creates a false impression of what a person is able to do. Time can't be managed, time is uncontrollable we can only manage ourselves and our use of time

Time management is actually self management. Its interesting that the skills we need to manage others are the same skills we need to manage ourselves: the ability to plan, delegate, organize, direct and control There are common time wasters which need to be identified. In order for a time management process to work it is important to know what aspects of our personal management need to be improved. Below you will find some of the most frequent reasons for reducing effectiveness in the workplace. Tick the ones which are causing to be the major obstacles to your own time management. These we refer to as your "Time Stealers". Identifying your time stealers:

- Interruptions—telephone

- Interruptions—personal visitors

- Meetings

- Tasks you should have delegated

- Procrastination and indecision

- Acting with incomplete information

- Dealing with team members

- Crisis management (fire fighting)

- Unclear communication

- Inadequate technical knowledge

- Unclear objectives and priorities

- Lack of planning

- Stress and fatigue

- Inability to say "No"

- Desk management and personal disorganization

Fortunately there are strategies you can use to manage your time, be more in control and reduce stress, but you can analyze your time and see how you may be both the cause and the solution to your time challenges. Below, we examine time management issues in more detail:

- Shifting priorities and crisis management. Crisis management is actually the form of management preferred by most managers. The irony is that actions taken prior to the crisis could have prevented the fire in the first place.

- The telephone. Have you ever had one of those days when you thought your true calling was in Telemarketing. The telephone-our greatest communication tool can be our biggest enemy to effectiveness if you don't know how to control its hold over you.

- Lack of priorities/objectives. This probably the biggest/most important time waster. It affects all we do both professionally and personally. Those who accomplish the most in a day know exactly what they want to accomplish. Unfortunately too many of us think that goals and objectives are yearly things and not daily considerations. This results in too much time spent on the minor things and not on the things which are important to our work/lives

- Attempting too much. Many people today feel that they have to accomplish everything yesterday and don't give themselves enough time to do things properly. This leads only to half finished projects and no feeling of achievement.

- Drop in visitors. The five deadliest words that rob your time are "Have you got a minute". Everyone's the culprit-colleagues., the boss, your peers. Knowing how to deal with interruptions is one of the best skills you can learn.

- Ineffective delegation. Good delegation is considered a key skill in both managers and leaders. The best managers have an ability to delegate work to staff and ensure it is done correctly. This is probably the best way of building a teams moral and reducing your workload at the same time. The general rule is-this; if one of your staff can do it 80% as well as you can, then delegate it.

- The cluttered desk. When you have finished reading this article look at your desk. If you can see less than 80% of it then you are probably suffering from 'desk stress'. The most effective people work from clear desks.

- Procrastination. The biggest thief of time; not decision making but decision avoidance. By reducing the amount of procrastinating you do you can substantially increase the amount of active time available to you.

- The inability to say "no!". The general rule is; if people can dump their work or problems on to your shoulders they will do it. Some of the most stressed people around lack the skill to 'just say no' for fear of upsetting people.

- Meetings. Studies have shown that the average manager spends about 17 hours a week in meetings and about 6 hours in the planning time and untold hours in the follow up. I recently spoke to an executive who has had in the last 3 months 250 meetings It is widely acknowledged that about as much of a third of the time spent in meetings is wasted due to poor meeting management and lack of planning If you remember your goal is to increase your self management, these are the best ways to achieve this;

There are many ways we can manage our time. We have listed some strategies you can use to manage your time.

- Always define your objectives as clearly as possible.

- Do you find you are not doing what you want because your goals have not been set. One of the factors which mark out successful people is their ability to work out what they want to achieve and have written goals which they can review them constantly. Your long term goals should impact on your daily activities and be included on your "to do" list. Without a goal or objective people tend to just drift personally and professionally

- Analyze your use of time. Are you spending enough time on the projects which although may not be urgent now are the things you need to do to develop yourself or your career. If you are constantly asking yourself "What is the most important use of my time, right now?" it will help you to focus on 'important tasks' and stop reacting to tasks which seem urgent (or pleasant to do) but carry no importance towards your goals.

- Have a plan. How can you achieve your goals without a plan. Most people know what they want but have no plan to achieve it except by sheer hard work. Your yearly plan should be reviewed daily and reset as your achievements are met. Successful people make lists constantly. It enables them to stay on top of priorities and enable them to remain flexible to changing priorities. This should be done for both personal and business goals.

- Action plan analysis. Problems will always occur, the value of a good plan is to identify them early and seek out solutions. Good time management enables you to measure the progress towards your goals because "What you can measure, you can control". Always try to be proactive.

Time management (or self management) is not a hard subject to understand, but unless you are committed to build time management techniques into your daily routine you'll only achieve partial (or no) results and then make comments such as "I tried time management once and it doesn't work for me". The lesson to learn is that the more time we spend planning our time and activities the more time we will have for those activities. By setting goals and eliminating time wasters and doing this everyday you may find you will have extra time in the week to spend on those people and activities most important to you.

The web is a fantastic place for marketing and promotion but there should be access to free information which is in abundance on many sites. Total Success have searched the web for free information on time management and you can find these on our time management links page. If you have more sites which contain relevant information or to inform me that a particular site does no longer exist (many sites come and go at a fast rate on the web), please e-mail us. The criteria for inclusion is a site which has a lot of free information on time management and not companies promoting time management courses or products.

6

Communication

Communication is arguably the most valuable skill that you can develop. Some of the top leaders, performers, and salespeople seem to have this seemingly elusive trait and likeability. The definition of charisma is allowing people to feel good about themselves while they are in your presence. Some people say that you are either born with it or not—but this is not true. You can develop your own personal charisma and make a huge impact on your business by developing the relationships that you keep with your employees/clients/business associates.

Communication skills are often over-looked. If you can not communicate your thoughts, ideas, and desires to those who can help you put the into practice, the you have no chance to be successful. Successful communication is the foundation of your plans.

Communicating at all levels is the key to successful communication. It does you no good if you can communicate with other managers, but you can not connect with the labor staff that actually completes the work. In reverse, as you work your way up the ladder, you may have great communication skills and respect at the field or labor level, but if you struggle with communication up the ladder, then you will not be successful either.

Communication should be a constantly evolving skill that you need to continually improve. You can never become too good of a communicator. Remember, however, that it is a two way street. Communication is more than clearly conveying your thoughts and ideas, it is also receiving and understanding the thoughts and ideas of others at all levels.

Listening With Full Attention

When an employee or coworker approaches you for advice, inspiration, feedback or a discussion, listen to understand what the individual needs from you. If you can't fully attend to the staff person at the minute for any reason, it is better to reschedule the conversation. If you are, for example, on your way to a meeting, struggling with a deadline, trying to leave early, or experiencing any other distraction, it is better to make an appointment when you can really listen to the person. Don't try to half way pay attention. You insult the person; you will never fully comprehend their position or need. Worst, the employee walks away feeling that you don't care about his or her concerns. It is far better to reschedule

Listening to Understand

Listen with your full attention directed toward understanding what your coworker or staff member needs from you. Many managers, especially, are so used to helping people solve problems that their first course of action is to begin brainstorming solutions and giving advice. Maybe the employee just needs a listening ear. Your best approach is to listen deeply, ask questions for clarification to make sure you understand the situation and then, only then, ask the person what they would like from you. Trust me. They usually know, and often, they breathe a sigh of relief and say, "Thanks for listening.

How to Hold a Difficult Conversation

If you manage people, work in Human Resources, or care about your friends at work, chances are good that one day you will need to hold a difficult conversation.

People dress inappropriately and unprofessionally for work. Personal hygiene is sometimes unacceptable. Flirtatious behavior can lead to a sexual harassment problem. A messy desk is not the sign of an organized mind. Unreturned pop cans do draw ants.

Vulgar language is unprofessional. Revealing cleavage belongs in a club, a party, or on the beach. Leaving dirty dishes for others to wash is rude. Have you encountered any of these examples? They're just samples of the types of behavior that cry out for responsible feedback. These steps will help you hold difficult conversations when people need professional feedback.

Seek permission to provide the feedback.

Even if you are the employee's boss, start by stating you have some feedback you'd like to share. Ask if it's a good time or if the employee would prefer to select another time and place. (Within reason, of course.)

- Use a soft entry. Don't dive right into the feedback—give the person a chance to brace for potentially embarrassing feedback. Tell the employee that you need to provide feedback that is difficult to share. If you're uncomfortable with your role in the conversation, you might say that, too. Most people are as uncomfortable providing feedback about an individual's personal dress or habits, as the person receiving the feedback.

- Often, you are in the feedback role because other employees have complained to you about the habit, behavior, or dress. Do not give in to the temptation to amplify the feedback, or excuse your responsibility for the feedback, by stating that a number of coworkers have complained. This heightens the embarrassment and harms the recovery of the person receiving feedback.

- The best feedback is straightforward and simple. Don't beat around the bush. I am talking with you because this is an issue that you need to address for success in this organization.

- Tell the person the impact that changing his or her behavior will have from a positive perspective. Tell the employee how choosing to do nothing will affect their career and job.

- Reach agreement about what the individual will do to change their behavior. Set a due date—tomorrow, in some cases. Set a time frame to review progress in others.

- Follow-up. The fact that the problem exists means that backsliding is possible; further clarification may also be necessary. Then, more feedback and possibly, disciplinary action are possible next steps.

Speaking Well

Do you speak too quickly or too slowly? People listen at a certain rate. If you speak faster or slower than they are listening, they will not retain your message as well. Keep regional differences in mind—what seems too fast in the South may not be in New York City. Pay attention to what you say and how you say it.

Fillers are, like, you know, annoying. When you hear yourself using uh, um, like, you know, and other similar fillers, it is usually a stall because your mouth got ahead of your brain. Slow down and concentrate on what you are saying.

Make powerful statements? You will sound uncertain and lack credibility if your voice goes "up" at the end of sentences. To see what I mean, ask a question out loud. Do you hear how your voice goes "up" at the end, in anticipation of an answer? Now, say, "I am an excellent speaker." Did that also sound like a question? If so, work on making your speech stronger.

Strong speech does not mean vulgar speech. If you frequently pepper your speech with profanity, clean it up a little bit. No one will be offended if you don't swear, but some will be if you do.

Do you interrupt others? Calm down and let them speak. Really listen to them, don't just wait for them to take a breath so you can jump in.

Modulate your volume. If you speak too quietly, it will be difficult for others to hear you. If you speak too loudly, it can be jarring.

Look at people when you speak to them. It is polite, and makes it easier for them to hear you. This is especially important for those who have a hearing loss, but will help everyone to better understand you.

Watch for verbal cues to see if your message is getting through. Is the person nodding, or do they look confused? Are they fidgeting or looking past you? Those could be signs that they aren't getting it or they aren't interested.

Remember that much of your message is delivered non-verbally. Your posture, facial expressions, gestures, even the way you are dressed, all affect how your message is received and interpreted.

Your message is important, so deliver it with importance.

7

Meeting Management

The importance of meetings can not be overlooked. I'm sure you have all seen the cartoon going around depicting meetings as the great alternative to actually working. Unfortunately about 85% of the time this cartoon is accurate. The number one reason people call meetings is because they are clueless as to how to resolve an issue. So they call a meeting of as many people as they can, and present the problem for discussion with hopes that someone will offer the solution to the problem, and then this person takes this solution and implements it as their own.

When confronted with calling a meeting, justify the meeting with one of these reasons, or do not call the meeting:

1.   inform everyone of potential actions,

2.   develop an understanding of issues and consequences, and

3.   reach agreement for taking the actions that will ultimately affect the community.

A single meeting cannot always satisfy all those purposes. This is especially true if the commission is considering a very large project or plan. The group interaction will need to occur in a series of different kinds of meetings. Here is a brief list of the kinds of meetings in which planning staff and often planning commissioners participate.

Types of Meetings

1. Sharing information and monitoring

This is often termed "telling and selling." An example is a neighborhood meeting in which a new program of neighborhood-level grants is first announced. A second example might be a meeting between planning staff and a developer to conduct an informal review of a project proposal.

2. Decision making and problem solving

These meetings are called "probing and exploring." Here, the end result of the meeting is not known, but the purpose is. The group has identified a problem and, through discussion, better defines the problem and begins to identify solutions. An example is the parks and recreation department meeting with youth-related agencies to discuss how to improve youth recreation programs.

3. Creative/idea-generating

In these meetings a designated group finds the solution. An example might be a meeting of middle school youth and staff that explores youth recreation needs and their solutions. Staff facilitates the meeting, and city council members and planning commissioners serve as sounding boards.

4. Social and ceremonial

No real business is conducted in these meetings, rather the purpose may be to end a project. Examples are meetings to bestow historic preservation awards, honor retiring planning commissioners, or celebrate the opening of a new park.

5. Legislative/administrative

These meetings are formal and result in decisions that are upheld by law. In some states, planning commissions may serve as quasi-judicial or administrative entities, with final decision-making authority, as in the approval of a final plat of a subdivision or a conditional use. More typically, the city council or other elected body is the legislative body and makes the legally binding decisions for the community. A city council meeting is a legislative meeting. In some communities, quasi-judicial or administrative decisions by planning commissions or boards of zoning appeals may be appealed to the legislative body.

6. Advisory

Most planning commission meetings are advisory. Although the decisions reached by the advisory group are not legally binding, the meetings are still conducted in a formal manner and follow proper rules of order. The advice developed through this meeting is presented formally to the legislative group. All decisions and recommendations are carefully documented. Sometimes a planning commission will meet with the city council to discuss joint expectations and to review commission recommendations over the past year.

Common Meeting Management Problems

Some meetings will combine the functions outlined above. In a planning process, it is also common for meetings to be done in stages as the planning progresses. Also, make certain you know when these meetings must be public and when they can be more informal and involve only certain parties. Sunshine or open meetings laws or requirements in a municipal charter affect meeting location, notice, and content.

The size of the group will affect how you interact and what you will enact. As a rule, the larger the group, the more formal and carefully planned a meeting must be. Large groups cannot accommodate open-ended discussion well. Undoubtedly, your planning commission already has administrative rules or bylaws for how it conducts its meetings. Make certain you know what they say. Review them carefully with your senior staff to ensure your meetings meet legal requirements. For more information on the legal requirements of conducting planning commission meetings, see "You Be the Judge," *The Commissioner*, Summer 1996.

Confusion may arise when planning commission meetings are used to solve problems. As much as possible for major issues, hold working meetings and well-facilitated public meetings prior to the commission meeting to allow for genuine problem solving to occur. Often the commission meeting itself is too late in the process to try and get substantial public input on major projects. For more routine hearings, public input at the planning commission meeting works fine.

Debra Stein, a San Francisco consultant who works with developers to guide their projects through the review and adoption process, has written a book on meeting management. From her perspective, a common problem with planning commission meetings that get out of control is the unrealistic expectations that everyone places on a single meeting. She believes it is unreasonable for the public and officials to think that the planning commission meeting is the place to resolve complex planning and development issues. Public involvement has to be addressed in a more comprehensive manner. Otherwise, the public may feel that its voice is being ignored.

Bill Lamont, AICP, a Denver planning consultant, adds that not all planning commission meetings are consensus-building meetings. There are times decisions will be made that do not please segments of the population. The decisions must be made in the best interest of the community as a whole. As long as the planning process has been thorough and fair, and it garners adequate community support, the planning decisions made by the commission have a good chance of holding over time. Planning commissioners must be prepared for the controversy and the occasional lack of consensus.

Preparation

One key to well run meetings is good preparation. Every meeting must:

Begin with the agenda. In planning commission meetings, staff and the commission chair create the agenda. The agenda must be available to the public and distributed to the commissioners and key participants sufficiently in advance of the meeting. It should identify the location of the meeting, the date, and start and end times.

A useful addition to an agenda is the time at which each item on the agenda will begin and end. As much as possible, the chair should adhere to the time schedule. A common problem is not setting time limits for discussion, resulting in overly long discussions. When this happens, you lose the attention of your fellow commissioners and participants. Therefore, setting and keeping time limits is important. If you set limits on presentations and comments, make certain everyone knows the time limit rule. Publish the time limits and the meeting management rules so speakers can prepare their remarks.

Orient new members and public attendees. The public should be oriented at the beginning of the meeting by the chair. The chair should review the principal rules of conduct, the purpose of the meeting, and the manner in which it will be conducted. Orientation for commissioners should occur in a separate meeting. Part of any orientation should include discussions of:

- The roles of chair, commissioners, staff, public, and presenter.

- The basis on which decisions are made and what documents guide decisions, such as the local comprehensive plan, zoning and subdivision ordinances, and state enabling legislation.

- The decisions the planning commission is authorized to make.

- Rules of conduct for meetings.

- Ethics and rules of official conduct for commissioners.

- Provide the commission with staff-prepared background materials prior to the meeting. It is crucial that commissioners read this material before the meeting and be prepared to speak to it. Here is what staff should provide as background materials:

  - Agenda
  - Proposal and copies of site plans and where appropriate, elevations of projects.
  - A staff report that provides:
    1. A review of local ordinance requirements pertinent to the proposal.
    2. An analysis of site conditions.
    3. Relevant materials in the local comprehensive plan.
    4. Comments or suggestions from other local government departments.
    5. A recommendation.

Running the meeting

A meeting must be led. The chair must:

1. move the meeting along to a successful conclusion,

2. make certain all items on the agenda are addressed, and

3. maintain order.

The chair convenes the meeting on time and, if possible, ends on time. This establishes the discipline for the meeting.

The chair also sets the tone of the meeting. This tone helps maintain order and respect for the process. The chair should:

- Be well briefed on all issues (he or she must do the homework).

- Project a sense of order, discipline, and dignity while remaining calm and impartial.

- Avoid taking sides on an issue while in the role of chair. The chair will typically vote last in a decision by the commission.

- Insist that everyone speak politely and in an orderly fashion; name calling, personal attacks, noisy outbreaks, and rude behavior must not be tolerated.

- Make certain that the meeting follows the legal requirements.

- Make certain that decisions are based on the information before the commission.

- Ensure that the reasons for the decisions are well documented and relate clearly to the comprehensive plan and relevant ordinances.

- Ensure that everyone has a reasonable opportunity to be heard without dominating the proceedings.

- Ensure the meeting is objective and fair to all parties.

The chair's role is not the only important role. Being a good follower as a commissioner is also critical. Most of the same rules apply: be well prepared, help maintain an orderly and fair meeting, substantiate opinions based on the planning documents and data.

The meeting is conducted by the commission and with public input. Staff members are active prior to the meeting, preparing materials for the commission; at the meeting, they are typically responsible for introducing the project and the staff report with recommendations. To do this, they may use slides or other visuals. Visual materials, including maps, plans, slides, and graphics, must be clear and intelligible. The planning director and commission chair should work together with other staff members to set a high standard for these presentations. Finally, presentations should be systematic and thorough, but not tedious in their detail. Copies of relevant information should be readily accessible to the public.

Developers or other presenters also have a role. Most often their projects are presented by staff, but they may be given an opportunity to comment or respond to questions. If the developer presents his or her own project, the same guidelines stated above apply.

The public is invited to listen and comment during planning commission meetings. The chair should make it clear when these comments are welcome and how they should be made. For example, the chair explains that speakers must use the microphone in order that their comments be recorded and heard throughout the room. Again, the chair sets time limits and enforces them.

If your commission does not have clear administrative rules for meetings, it is strongly suggested that you adopt some. Consult your local government attorney about questions of procedural due process and complying with statutes or local ordinance or charter requirements. Your meeting management policies can reach far beyond legal issues and address issues such as visual documentation, time limits, maintaining order, etc.

Recording the actions

Planning commission meetings must be recorded. The secretary shapes the information into a written record. Minutes must be made available to commissioners and the public in a timely fashion. Some communities use their web site as a way of keeping the public informed. Posting minutes in a public area is also a good idea.

The decisions that the commission makes must be clearly written and properly substantiated.

Doing four simple things right during your meetings would reduce the time managers spend in meetings by 80 percent.

1.   Start on time

2.   Follow a detailed agenda

3.   Prioritize the agenda items so that you address the most important first.

4.   End on time

- Meeting Follow-up

If you think that distributing minutes with assigned action items and due dates will make your meetings effective, think again. My long experience is that many meeting participants fail to look at the minutes until the day of the next meeting. (This assumes that the meeting recorder distributed the minutes before the day of the next meeting—another frequent by-product of busy work lives.) To make meeting follow-up work, you need to develop a culture of accountability that makes it not okay to show up at the next meeting with action items incomplete. Barring a culture change, the meeting leader needs to follow-up with participants regularly between meetings to ensure action items are under way. (Yes, someone cares and is asking.)

8

Team Building

Employee involvement is creating an environment in which people have an impact on decisions and actions that affect their jobs. Employee involvement is not the goal nor is it a tool, as practiced in many organizations. Rather, it is a management and leadership philosophy about how people are most enabled to contribute to continuous improvement and the ongoing success of their work organization.

From working with people for many years, I have found that it is important to involve people as much as possible in all aspects of work decisions and planning. This involvement increases ownership and commitment, retains your best employees, and fosters an environment in which people choose to be motivated and contributing. It is also important for team building. People want to know that they are making a difference.

How to involve employees in decision-making and continuous improvement activities is the strategic aspect of involvement and can include such methods as suggestion systems, manufacturing cells, work teams, continuous improvement meetings, events, corrective action processes and periodic discussions with the supervisor.

Intrinsic to most employee involvement processes is training in team effectiveness, communication, and problem solving; the development of reward and recognition systems; and frequently, the sharing of gains made through employee involvement efforts. The best and most simple way is to simply ask for someone's opinion. You'd be surprised how well they may respond to it.

Leadership and involvement includes increasing the role for employees and a decreasing the role for supervisors in the decision process.

- **Tell:** the supervisor makes the decision and announces it to staff. The supervisor provides complete direction. Tell is useful when communicating about safety issues, government regulations and for decisions that neither require nor ask for employee input.

- **Sell:** the supervisor makes the decision and then attempts to gain commitment from staff by "selling" the positive aspects of the decision. Sell is useful when employee commitment is needed, but the decision is not open to employee influence.

- **Consult:** the supervisor invites input into a decision while retaining authority to make the final decision herself. The key to a successful consultation is to inform employees, on the front end of the discussion, that their input is needed, but that the supervisor is retaining the authority to make the final decision. This is the level of involvement that can create employee dissatisfaction most readily when this is not clear to the people providing input.

- **Join:** the supervisor invites employees to make the decision with the supervisor. The supervisor considers his voice equal in the decision process. The key to a successful join is when the supervisor truly builds consensus around a decision and is willing to keep her influence equal to that of the others providing input.

- **Delegate:** the supervisor turns the decision over to another party. The key to successful delegation is to always build a feedback loop and a timeline into the process. The supervisor must also share any "preconceived picture" he has of the anticipated outcome of the process.

The members of every team and work group develop particular ways of interacting with each other over time. Effective interpersonal communication among members and successful communication with managers and employees external to the team are critical components of team functioning.

How a team makes decisions, assigns work, and holds members accountable determines team success. With the potential power of the impact of these interactions on team success, why leave team member interaction to chance? Form team relationship guidelines or team norms early to ensure team success.

Team norms are a set of rules or guidelines that a team establishes to shape the interaction of team members with each other and with employees who are external to the team. Team norms can be developed during an early team meeting.

More norms can be added as the team sees the need for additional guidelines. Once developed, team norms are used to guide team member behavior. Team norms are used to assess how well team members are interacting. Team norms enable team members to call each other out on any behavior that is dysfunctional or that is negatively impacting the success of the team.

People in every workplace talk about building the team, working as a team, and my team, but few understand how to create the experience of team work or how to develop an effective team. Belonging to a team, in the broadest sense, is a result of feeling part of something larger than yourself. It has a lot to do with your understanding of the mission or objectives of your organization.

In a team-oriented environment, you contribute to the overall success of the organization. You work with fellow members of the organization to produce these results. Even though you have a specific job function and you belong to a specific department, you are unified with other organization members to accomplish the overall objectives. The bigger picture drives your actions; your function exists to serve the bigger picture.

You need to differentiate this overall sense of teamwork from the task of developing an effective intact team that is formed to accomplish a specific goal. Executives, managers and organization staff members universally explore ways to improve business results and profitability. Many view team-based, horizontal, organization structures as the best design for involving all employees in creating business success.

No matter what you call your team-based improvement effort: continuous improvement, total quality, lean manufacturing or self-directed work teams, you are striving to improve results for customers. Few organizations, however, are totally pleased with the results their team improvement efforts produce. If your team improvement efforts are not living up to your expectations, this self-diagnosing checklist may tell you why. Successful team building, that creates effective, focused work teams, requires attention to each of the following.

- **Clear Expectations:** Has executive leadership clearly communicated its expectations for the team's performance and expected outcomes? Do team members understand why the team was created? Is the organization demonstrating constancy of purpose in supporting the team with resources of people, time and money? Does the work of the team receive sufficient emphasis as a priority in terms of the time, discussion, attention and interest directed its way by executive leaders?

- **Context:** Do team members understand why they are participating on the team? Do they understand how the strategy of using teams will help the organization attain its communicated business goals? Can team members define their team's importance to the accomplishment of corporate goals? Does the team understand where its work fits in the total context of the organization's goals, principles, vision and values?

- **Commitment:** Do team members want to participate on the team? Do team members feel the team mission is important? Are members committed to accomplishing the team mission and expected outcomes? Do team members perceive their service as valuable to the organization and to their own careers? Do team members anticipate recognition for their contributions? Do team members expect their skills to grow and develop on the team? Are team members excited and challenged by the team opportunity?

- **Competence:** Does the team feel that it has the appropriate people participating? (As an example, in a process improvement, is each step of the process represented on the team?) Does the team feel that its members have the knowledge, skill and capability to address the issues for which the team was formed? If not, does the team have access to the help it needs? Does the team feel it has the resources, strategies and support needed to accomplish its mission?

- **Charter:** Has the team taken its assigned area of responsibility and designed its own mission, vision and strategies to accomplish the mission.

- **Control:** Does the team have enough freedom and empowerment to feel the ownership necessary to accomplish its charter? At the same time, do team members clearly understand their boundaries? How far may members go in pursuit of solutions? Are limitations (i.e. monetary and time resources) defined at the beginning of the project before the team experiences barriers and rework?

Is the team's reporting relationship and accountability understood by all members of the organization? Has the organization defined the team's authority? To make recommendations? To implement its plan? Is there a defined review process so both the team and the organization are consistently aligned in direction and purpose? Do team members hold each other accountable for project timelines.

commitments and results? Does the organization have a plan to increase opportunities for self-management among organization members?

- **Collaboration:** Does the team understand team and group process? Do members understand the stages of group development? Are team members working together effectively interpersonally? Do all team members understand the roles and responsibilities of team members? team leaders? team recorders? Can the team approach problem solving, process improvement, goal setting and measurement jointly? Do team members cooperate to accomplish the team charter? Has the team established group norms or rules of conduct in areas such as conflict resolution, consensus decision making and meeting management? Is the team using an appropriate strategy to accomplish its action plan?

- **Communication:** Are team members clear about the priority of their tasks? Is there an established method for the teams to give feedback and receive honest performance feedback? Does the organization provide important business information regularly? Do the teams understand the complete context for their existence? Do team members communicate clearly and honestly with each other? Do team members bring diverse opinions to the table? Are necessary conflicts raised and addressed?

- **Creative Innovation:** Is the organization really interested in change? Does it value creative thinking, unique solutions, and new ideas? Does it reward people who take reasonable risks to make improvements? Or does it reward the people who fit in and maintain the status quo? Does it provide the training, education, access to books and films, and field trips necessary to stimulate new thinking?

- **Consequences:** Do team members feel responsible and accountable for team achievements? Are rewards and recognition supplied when teams are successful? Is reasonable risk respected and encouraged in the organization? Do team members fear reprisal? Do team members spend their time finger pointing rather than resolving problems? Is the organization designing reward systems that recognize both team and individual performance? Is the organization planning to share gains and increased profitability with team and individual contributors? Can contributors see their impact on increased organization success?

- **Coordination:** Are teams coordinated by a central leadership team that assists the groups to obtain what they need for success? Have priorities and resource allocation been planned across departments? Do teams understand the concept of the internal customer—the next process, anyone to whom they provide a product or a service? Are cross-functional and multi-department teams common and working together effectively? Is the organization developing a customer-focused process-focused orientation and moving away from traditional departmental thinking?

- **Cultural Change:** Does the organization recognize that the team-based, collaborative, empowering, enabling organizational culture of the future is different than the traditional, hierarchical organization it may currently be? Is the organization planning to or in the process of changing how it rewards, recognizes, appraises, hires, develops, plans with, motivates and manages the people it employs?

Does the organization plan to use failures for learning and support reasonable risk? Does the organization recognize that the more it can change its climate to support teams, the more it will receive in pay back from the work of the teams?

Spend time and attention on each of these twelve tips to ensure your work teams contribute most effectively to your business success.

9

Training and Development

Definite advantages exist for your organization when you have developed the training capabilities of your managers. Teach managers to train and you will increase the effectiveness of your internal training. Additionally, training and mentoring become a more expected and utilized part of the managers' jobs. Employees react positively when managers provide training, too. The employees believe they will have the opportunity to use the training; they react more positively to the expectations of the manager versus a trainer. When they provide training, managers are enabled to articulate what they believe is important and to reinforce these ideas with employees. Employees are impressed that the training topic is so important that the manager takes the time to do the training.

Definite advantages exist for your organization when you have developed the training capabilities of your employees. Teach employees to train and you will increase the effectiveness of your internal training. Employees are familiar with the workings—both good and bad—of your internal organization. They should be familiar with the goals, the culture or environment, the company strengths, the company weaknesses, and the actual employees. This gives employees an advantage over a trainer who has to learn about the culture, the company strengths, the company weaknesses, and also get to know the people.

Use existing employees to train new employees during the new employee orientation. A long term sales representative can train all new sales employees about the sales customer relationship management, computer programs, cold calling and prospecting, and how to take and process orders. In the same company, a shipping employee could train, test, and certify all delivery drivers.

When an employee attends a conference, seminar or educational event of any kind, the transfer of the knowledge gained to the workplace is essential. It's also the hardest part of training and development. Employees must use the ideas obtained in the training session immediately upon their return to work. Use it or lose it is a standard saying in the training field. It's a correct statement. The employee must be expected to demonstrate the use of the training in a work environment that supports the use of the training. Most powerful? It helps if the boss asks, "What did you learn in the training—and what do you plan to do differently, now that you've learned it?"

In a usual approach to training, meet with groups weekly for a short training session. These sessions can last for several years, although we need to limit the frequency over time.

The key to the success of the training sessions is that the time together, the discussion, the shared training topics, the new information, and the shared reading both educate and build the team. Additionally, learning comes in bites small enough to practice and participants are not overwhelmed with information. They also have the chance to discuss what worked at the next training session.

It takes anywhere from three to 15 months to find the right job—yet just days or weeks to lose it. Here are 10 trainable traits that are career poison:

1. Possessing Poor People Skills
    A little likeability can go a long way. Studies by both the Harvard Business Review and Fast Company magazine show that people consistently and overwhelmingly prefer to work with likeable, less-skilled co-workers than with highly competent jerks. Researchers found that if employees are disliked, it's almost irrelevant whether they're good at what they do, because other workers will avoid them.

2. Not Being a Team Player
    No one feels comfortable around a prima Donna. And organizations have ways of dealing with employees who subvert the team. Just ask Philadelphia Eagles Wide Receiver Terrell Owens, who was suspended for the 2005 season after repeatedly clashing and taking public shots at his teammates and management. Show you're a team player by making your boss look like a star and demonstrating that you've got the greater good of the organization at heart.

3. Missing Deadlines
    If the deadline is Wednesday, first thing Thursday won't cut it. Organizations need people they can depend on. Missing deadlines is not only unpro-

fessional, it can play havoc with others' schedules and make your boss look bad. When making commitments, it's best to under-promise and over-deliver. Then, pull an all-nighter if you have to. It's that important.

4. Conducting Personal Business on Company Time
    The company e-mail and phone systems are for company business. Keep personal phone calls brief and few—and never take a call that will require a box of tissues to get through. Also, never type anything in an e-mail that you don't want read by your boss; many systems save deleted messages to a master file. And we can't tell you how many poor souls have gotten fired for hitting the "Reply All" button and disseminating off-color jokes—or worse yet—rants about their boss for all to see.

5. Isolating Yourself
    Don't isolate yourself. Develop and use relationships with others in your company and profession. Those who network effectively have an inside track on resources and information and can more quickly cut through organizational politics. Research shows effective net workers tend to serve on more successful teams, get better performance reviews, receive more promotions and be more highly compensated.

6. Starting an Office Romance
    Unless you're in separate locations, office romances are a bad idea. If you become involved with your boss, your accomplishments and promotions will be suspect; if you date a subordinate, you leave yourself open to charges of sexual harassment. And if it ends badly, you're at risk of everyone knowing about it and witnessing the unpleasantness.

7. Fearing Risk or Failure
    If you don't believe in yourself, no one else will. Have a can-do attitude and take risks. Instead of saying, "I've never done that," say, "I'll learn how." Don't be afraid to fail or make mistakes. If you do mess up, admit it and move on. Above all, find the learning opportunities in every situation. Remember, over time, risk-aversion can be more hazardous to your career than error.

8. Having No Goals
    Failure doesn't lie in not reaching your goal, but in not having a goal to reach. Set objectives and plan your daily activities around achieving them.

Eighty percent of your effectiveness comes from 20 percent of your activities. Manage your priorities and focus on those tasks that support your goals.

9.   Neglecting Your Image
Fair or not, appearance counts. People draw all kinds of conclusions from the way you present yourself. So don't come to work poorly groomed or in inappropriate attire. Be honest, use proper grammar and avoid slang and expletives. You want to project an image of competence, character and commitment.

10. Being Indiscreet
Cubicles, hallways, email, elevators, bathrooms—even commuter trains—are not your private domain. Be careful where you hold conversations and what you say to whom. Don't tell off-color jokes, reveal company secrets, gossip about co-workers or espouse your views on race, religion or the boss' personality. Because while there is such a thing as free speech, it's not so free if it costs you your job!

Remembering that all of your employees want to advance and become successful, the most important concept to remember and to preach to your staff is that none of them can be promoted to the next level until they train their replacement to take their place. This concept helps the company by continuously promoting coaching and mentoring, as well as helping the individual employees by teaching them how to function at the level of their individual boss every day.

10

Motivation

Values play a defining role in motivation. An organization that has identified and examined the values by which people want to live is a workplace with motivation potential. Values such as integrity, empowerment, perseverance, equality, discipline and accountability, when truly integrated in the culture of the organization, are powerful motivators. They become the compass that the organization uses to select staff members, reward and recognize employees' performance and guide interaction among staff members. If you work in an organization that values empowerment, for example, you are unafraid to take thoughtful risks. You are likely to identify and solve problems. You are comfortable making decisions without a supervisor looking over your shoulder. The downside to identifying values occurs when an organization's leaders claim certain values and then behave in ways that are contradictory to the stated values.

In these workplaces, values deflate motivation because employees don't trust their leaders' word.

As managers, CEOs, Presidents, Executives, Vice Presidents all have a bad habit of forgetting where they came from, and forgetting what it was like to be in the trenches everyday. Executives have a tendency to feel that they are entitled to disproportionately more than the people actually getting the work done. This is the number one motivation killer for employees. If you do any of the following things, you are de-motivating your people and setting yourself up for high turnover, insubordination, disrespect and ultimate failure.

- If you set your expense accounts more than twice as high as your employees. If you give your employees an entertainment meal budget of $200.00 per month, yours better not be more than $400.0 per month.

- Company vehicles should not have different levels of status. Provide the best vehicle to enable the employee to efficiently get their job done. In other words, don't give a service mechanic a pickup when he needs a van, or a salesman a car when they need an SUV. At the same time, there is no need for executives to be driving exotic cars. This simply raises overhead and demoralizes the troops.

- Board meetings, strategic planning meetings and any executive type meetings need to be held in the company conference rooms. Taking a trip somewhere under the guise of having meetings is simply stealing a vacation from the company under the excuse of a meeting. No one buys the argument that you need to get executive level meetings out of the office. We all know it is crap.

- Never ask anyone in the organization to do anything that you would not do yourself. And if it is something that you can not do, because you do not possess the technical skills, then don't try to portray that you can do it. Admit that you can not do it and hat you value those in the organization that can do it. You may be surprised to find that people leave supervisors more often than they leave jobs. Thinking about motivation, here are some of the supervisory actions that cause people to leave their jobs.

- You need to pay attention to employees and help them feel important. This involved asking them how they are doing, thanking them for their efforts and keeping commitments to them.

- Keeping commitments is as simple as attending a scheduled meeting rather than postponing it because everything else is more important.

- Recognition is a key factor in employee motivation and people like to hear words of praise from their boss.

- You need to provide solid direction so your staff knows that they are accomplishing important goals; the power of feedback cannot be overemphasized.

- Provide staff the opportunity to learn, grow and make career progress.

- Finally, help employees feel like members of the "in-crowd". They want to know what is happening as quickly as everyone else—earlier, if possible. Do these activities wisely and you'll be viewed as a positive, motivating supervisor and you'll keep your best staff

How can you help a colleague or reporting staff member choose motivation? You take steps to create a work environment that provides the greatest possibility for employees to choose motivation. A motivating work environment provides a simple framework so people know what is expected from them.

Employees don't do what they're supposed to do because they don't know what they are supposed to do. Lacking the necessary direction, employees are unclear about their personal goals and objectives. The organization feels rudderless. Or, worse, the goals and direction change daily. The employees scramble to switch gears and the result is often too many goals, no priority placed on the existing goals and the feeling that all of the goals, regardless of their importance, must be accomplished. When results are monitored, baby steps toward accomplishing each goal are evident, but no goals are completed. For a motivating work environment, a simple framework in which employees know the vision, mission, goals and action plans is required. Employees with strategic direction are motivated to succeed.

True motivation comes from within, from a person's own psyche, the innermost recesses of the soul, secret desires and deep-rooted needs which motivate, "push" us towards their satisfaction. What a manager can do is create an environment in which employees can feel motivated.

Many people go through life unaware of their "true calling", their "motivations". People abandoned early dreams to deal with life's realities making decisions based in need rather than motivation. They had to conform to society, family, the corporate world and other circles, each of which dictates its code of conduct: how to think, feel, eat, speak, behave and dress. Their true selves disappear, get buried. It is only by triggering and bringing out into the light people's nature, gifts and secret desires that we give them the opportunity to feel motivated. This is no attempt at playing the psychologist, but a rough explanation of some basic precepts.

All humans share basic needs that must be addressed, ranging from shelter to more sophisticated drives. All of these things are motivators that motivate us to do what we do, and make the decisions that we make.

Physiological Needs: Basic physical needs: the ability to acquire food, shelter, clothing and other basics to survive

Safety Needs: A safe and non-threatening work environment, job security, safe equipment and installations

Social Needs: Contact and friendship with fellow-workers, social activities and opportunities

Ego: Recognition, acknowledgment, rewards
Once basic needs are satisfied, people want more. Progress is the essence of human nature. When people's basic needs are addressed, their mind is free of threat and insecurity, and open up to some of their drives. People are often confused between "superficial wants" and "inner drives." Some individuals are in pursuit of material luxury, while others pursue their thirst for knowledge, artistic expression, a need to lead or help others, play the hero or shine in society.

Holding a basic understanding of this concept benefits the company if we discover who every worker is, his/her drives, special gifts, abilities, hopes and plans for the future. If we take time to discover this, understand what makes this person "tick", we will be able to utilize this worker in the position which is the best "fit", a step ahead towards employee motivation. We must also clarify management values, design and implement effective policies and techniques.

Every employee has a need for self-expression, entertains plans for professional development and career advancement, wishes to be accepted as "family member", feel respect towards management and pride in his/her work, receive acknowledgment and reward, be listened to and trusted. Through strategic communications (including meetings) our duty is to share with employees the company goals, market, industry and business information and future plans, and invite employees to give feedback. We must learn how to place people in a role where they can use their abilities and make progress towards the realization of personal goals. Misplacements can cause a company substantial financial loss due to turnover, accidents, lawsuits, rebates, refunds, loss of customers and sales.

We must learn how to create a corporate culture and a supportive work environment. This is done through leadership and management excellence, a human approach, effective human resources strategies, "positive discipline", fair and just treatment to all, clearly defined policies, career and personal development training programs (including cross-training and job rotation), career path identification, organizational communications, tools to facilitate communication, team assignments, reward programs, objective appraisals, adequate pay, benefits and company activities.

It is important for employees to know that management is aware of their exist- ence, recognizes them, remembers their names and greets them. Managers who fail to greet employees or respond to greetings lead to a high degree of de-motiva- tion, lack of trust, and disloyalty.

Individuals and departments need to be thanked for their hard work and special achievements and be rewarded for contributions. Managers who encourage employees to use initiative and set higher challenges for themselves achieve more positive results than those who cause employees to compete with each other. Per- sonal accomplishments at the expense of others, defeats team-work and nega- tively affects service to customers.

Managers can win over employees' loyalty and best input by treating them as "partners", showing care, listening to them and sharing, but this alone is only a part of the plan. According to a recent report by an international employee recruitment firm, employees (ages 18—25) expect employers to challenge them and give them ample opportunities to grow professionally. As well, 36% of these employees don't see themselves in the same job 2 years down the road.

Meeting the demands of this new generation of employees is now at the top of the agenda for small and medium-sized businesses. As a manager, you'll have to motivate employees to stay loyal to your firm with more satisfying jobs, ongoing training and anything else that makes you stand out from your competitors.

Yet despite the popular belief that wooing employees is a costly venture for a businesses, the reality is that employee motivation can involve little or no cost.

Make the job motivating

Pressed for time, few managers take the time to prepare written job descriptions. However, experts agree that improvising is not a winning strategy. The more accurate and realistic you are about specifications and job requirements for the position, the more likely that your people will feel motivated to do a good job. It's important to:

- Get your employees involved in writing their job descriptions, so they feel they have genuine input.

- Put the emphasis on active, engaging verbs such as "analyzes", "sets up" or "operates."

- Build in clear goals so that employees can see visible progress and results.

- Ensure that the work is challenging enough for the employee: don't hire somebody with too many skills for the job. Generation Y employees don't like jobs that feel trivial.

- Give your employees enough leeway to be independent, which encourages personal and professional development.

- Compensate your employees based on their performance.

Give employees feedback

Feedback allows your employees to evolve, improve their skills and do more for your company. And that's why it's important to assess your employees' performance regularly and fairly. For starters, make sure they understand why performance feedback is necessary. Frank discussions will help obtain the best possible results but it's also vital to be diplomatic and flexible. Be open to suggestions that could improve the efficiency of your company's operations. Ensure that you:

- Be systematic about performance evaluation for every employee, no matter what level in your company.

- Link the performance evaluation to your compensation program, so that employees take it seriously.

- Give feedback often—both praise and constructive criticism.

- Mention positive aspects first, then difficult points, finishing with a solution or mentioning a positive action that may help.

- Encourage your employees to evaluate themselves. This gives you an accurate picture of how they view their performance. It can also reveal where improvement is needed.

- Establish realistic performance objectives for your employees and make sure they understand and agree.

- Rely on simple, ongoing feedback techniques, such as:

- personal congratulations for a job well-done
- personal notes from managers to mark a good performance
- recognizing employee performance and promotions in vehicles such as internal newsletters
- showing your team confidence so that even average performers feel motivated to give more

Manage your top performers

Your star performers may be a little more demanding than your average performers. They tend to leave companies if they feel they're not getting enough attention. Factor these points in:

- Give your top performers some leeway. Avoid micromanaging and give them the room to do their best.

- Get their input often. If you don't seek their ideas, they'll stop giving them to you.

- Reward excellent performance with extra perks. However, be modest and be careful not to create an atmosphere of resentment with massive bonuses, for example.

- Point out where they need to improve; you want to encourage even your best performers to strive harder.

- Praise top performers when they excel. Don't assume that they know they're doing a good job.

Give employees innovative perks

In today's demanding business world, many employees are looking for perks beyond monetary compensation, stock options and profit-sharing.

- Consider options such as flexible hours.

- Give employees "downtime" when they've worked hard. Employees tend to want perks such as more time off rather than more money.

- Allow employees to work at home.

Reinforce team spirit

The fact is motivated employees, who sing from the same song sheet, contribute their best. Keep these ideas in mind in order to reinforce team spirit.

- Encourage people to interact outside the office environment, i.e., dinners or sports events.

- Put employees at ease by holding informal gatherings at your home.

- Assign a buddy for new employees to help them during orientation.

- Avoid creating hierarchy by assigning perks such as more office space and free parking.

Most Important Point

Ultimately, last but not least, do not convince yourself that you are paying what the market dictates for your employees. I have worked for many managers that convince themselves that they pay competitively, and seek out information and comparisons to substantiate it, ignoring all information that does not substantiate their position.

Be honest about what the market is worth and pay it. I've worked for companies with such a skewed vision of their actions, that it is almost laughable. Here is the most common example closed minded management that happens every day:

A company has a top performing employee making $100k a year, and this employee is offered another position with a competitor making $115k a year. The management takes the position that they will not pay that extra $15k to retain that employee because they refuse to be held hostage to their employees.

In this case, management is missing the big picture, and will not pay a mere $15k to keep the best, most knowledgeable, top performers in your company? If you have someone in your company making $100k, they are likely responsible for millions in revenue, but somehow you justify the risk of sending this revenue with your ex-employee to your competitor. Next, by letting this key employee leave, you will need to hire someone in their place. You will end up paying at least $10k (because that is the market value) more to fill this position with someone who knows nothing about your company or clients. Not to mention the $10k—$20k cost of finding, hiring, and possibly relocating this person.

Somehow you've convinced yourself that the "market value" of employees is what you were paying, even though your competitors are paying more for the same people. Isn't that, by definition "market value"?

The bottom line is that if you believe that you can be held hostage by your employees, then you should not be in the position that you are in. Employees do not set the value of employees, competitive employers do, and that is the definition of "market value". It is always less expensive to keep top performers, than to send them to your competitors.

The most important thing to remember about motivation is that all employees are motivated by money. Everything else is secondary to money. Let me repeat that: Everything else is secondary to money. Your employee motivation strategies can be built into a sound human resources plan, but none of that matters if you are not willing to pay the value of your people.

11

Habits of Business Success

Learning and instilling new habits in your daily business life can have a dramatic effect on your level of success. Review each of the 7 habits. Choose one habit to focus on for a month or until you achieve mastery. Gradually incorporate each of the 7 habits of business success into your life and attain your business dreams.

Habit 1.

Managers practicing the art of business success know the power of networks. They take the time to identify and build relationships with key peers, mentors, and advisors. This inner network provides support, direction, and an increased number of people to assist. Having an inner network of five people who have a network of five more, grows the network exponentially.

Habit 2.

Customer Centric: Business success requires an unwavering commitment to the customer. This commitment encompasses a mindset of understanding the customers' world. Understanding the customers wants and needs provides the business with a greater opportunity to earn a loyal customer base. Focus away from business and profits, and toward what you can do to improve the life of your customers.

Habit 3.

Humble Honesty: Business success requires the ability to know your strengths and weaknesses. Being open and honest about yourself and your business creates growth as an individual and as a company. Don't spend time developing weaknesses. Find help for weak areas, enabling you to focus on strengths. In the book, "Now, Discover Your Strengths", Gallup Organization reveals that building our strengths instead of fixing our weakness is the path to mastery and success. Take the time to know yourself and business.

Habit 4.

Adaptability: Business success requires the ability to adapt to changing situations. Nothing ever goes as planned. The world of business is full of surprises and unforeseen events. Using the habit of adaptability allows business owners to respond to circumstances with the ability to change course and act without complete information. Being flexible allows us to respond to changes without being paralyzed with fear and uncertainty.

Habit 5.

Opportunity Focused: Problems are a regular part of business life. Staff issues, customer misunderstandings, cash crunches-the list is endless. To achieve business success, look at both sides of the coin. Every problem has an opportunity. Being opportunity focused makes the game of business fun and energizing.

Habit 6.

Finding A Better Way: Productivity is the cornerstone of business success. Formulate the habit of finding a better way to make your business more productive. This will create more time to focus on the critical issues that drive sales and profit. Productivity can be enhanced by technology, automation, outsourcing, and improving business processes.

Habit 7.

Balanced Lifestyle Management: A business can consume an owner's time and energy. It's easy to allow the business to take control of your life. Business success requires the habit of balancing all aspects of your life. Separating time for daily business tasks, profit driven tasks, and free time is a habit that will make your business and life more enjoyable. Take the time to plan each week.

APPENDIX

Sam Walton: 10 Rules for Building a Successful Business

Below is the 10 rules for building a successful business according to Sam Walton. I include this because if you have never read this it is worth reading, and if you have, it is worth reading again.

Sam Walton grew up poor during the Great Depression, yet rose to start the biggest retail store Wal-Mart. In Sam Walton's "Running a Successful Company: Ten Rules that Worked for Me," learn Walton's winning formula for business.

Sam Walton 1918—1992

Sam Walton, the founder of Wal-Mart, grew up poor in a farm community in rural Missouri during the Great Depression. The poverty he experienced while growing up taught him the value of money and to persevere.

After attending the University of Missouri, he immediately worked for J.C. Penny where he got his first taste of retailing. He served in World War II, after which he became a successful franchiser of Ben Franklin five-and-dime stores. In 1962, he had the idea of opening bigger stores, sticking to rural areas, keeping costs low and discounting heavily. The management disagreed with his vision. Undaunted, Walton pursued his vision, founded Wal-Mart and started a retailing success story. When Walton died in 1992, the family's net worth approached $25 billion.

Today, Wal-Mart is the world's #1 retailer, with more than 4,150 stores, including discount stores, combination discount and grocery stores, and membership-only warehouse stores (Sam's Club). Learn Walton's winning formula for business.

Rule 1:

Commit to your business. Believe in it more than anybody else. I think I overcame every single one of my personal shortcomings by the sheer passion I brought to my work. I don't know if you're born with this kind of passion, or if you can learn it. But I do know you need it. If you love your work, you'll be out there every day trying to do it the best you possibly can, and pretty soon everybody around will catch the passion from you—like a fever.

Rule 2:

Share your profits with all your associates, and treat them as partners. In turn, they will treat you as a partner, and together you will all perform beyond your wildest expectations. Remain a corporation and retain control if you like, but behave as a servant leader in your partnership. Encourage your associates to hold a stake in the company. Offer discounted stock, and grant them stock for their retirement. It's the single best thing we ever did.

Rule 3:

Motivate your partners. Money and ownership alone aren't enough. Constantly, day by day, think of new and more interesting ways to motivate and challenge your partners. Set high goals, encourage competition, and then keep score. Make bets with outrageous payoffs. If things get stale, cross-pollinate; have managers switch jobs with one another to stay challenged. Keep everybody guessing as to what your next trick is going to be. Don't become too predictable.

Rule 4:

Communicate everything you possibly can to your partners. The more they know, the more they'll understand. The more they understand, the more they'll care. Once they care, there's no stopping them. If you don't trust your associates to know what's going on, they'll know you really don't consider them partners. Information is power, and the gain you get from empowering your associates more than offsets the risk of informing your competitors.

Rule 5:

Appreciate everything your associates do for the business. A paycheck and a stock option will buy one kind of loyalty. But all of us like to be told how much somebody appreciates what we do for them. We like to hear it often, and especially when we have done something we're really proud of. Nothing else can quite substitute for a few well-chosen, well-timed, sincere words of praise. They're absolutely free—and worth a fortune.

Rule 6:

Celebrate your success. Find some humor in your failures. Don't take yourself so seriously. Loosen up, and everybody around you will loosen up. Have fun. Show enthusiasm—always. When all else fails, put on a costume and sing a silly song. Then make everybody else sing with you. Don't do a hula on Wall Street. It's been done. Think up your own stunt. All of this is more important, and more fun, than you think, and it really fools competition. "Why should we take those cornballs at Wal-Mart seriously?"

Rule 7:

Listen to everyone in your company and figure out ways to get them talking. The folks on the front lines—the ones who actually talk to the customer—are the only ones who really know what's going on out there. You'd better find out what they know. This really is what total quality is all about. To push responsibility down in your organization, and to force good ideas to bubble up within it, you must listen to what your associates are trying to tell you.

Rule 8:

Exceed your customer's expectations. If you do, they'll come back over and over. Give them what they want—and a little more. Let them know you appreciate them. Make good on all your mistakes, and don't make excuses—apologize. Stand behind everything you do. The two most important words I ever wrote were on that first Wal-Mart sign: "Satisfaction Guaranteed." They're still up there, and they have made all the difference.

Rule 9:

Control your expenses better than your competition. This is where you can always find the competitive advantage. For twenty-five years running—long before Wal-Mart was known as the nation's largest retailer—we've ranked No. 1 in our industry for the lowest ratio of expenses to sales. You can make a lot of different mistakes and still recover if you run an efficient operation. Or you can be brilliant and still go out of business if you're too inefficient.

Rule 10:

Swim upstream. Go the other way. Ignore the conventional wisdom. If everybody else is doing it one way, there's a good chance you can find your niche by going in exactly the opposite direction. But be prepared for a lot of folks to wave you down and tell you you're headed the wrong way. I guess in all my years, what I heard more often than anything was: a town of less than 50,000 population cannot support a discount store for very long.

About The Author

Nick Kasik currently lives in Las Vegas, NV with his wife Niki, and their three children, Megan, Amber & Alex. Nick grew up in a very rural Nebraska farming community that was rich on character and values, but poor on opportunity. So he put this work ethic to work for him and worked his way through college graduating with both an Associates degree in Heating and Air Conditioning, & a Bachelors degree in Mechanical Engineering. He then began a successful career in construction management with one of the top mechanical contracting firms in the country.

Along the way his drive and energy compelled him to take his love on street rods and motorcycles and turn his hobby into a successful business building custom motorcycles http://www.temptresschoppers.com./

Armed with the knowledge gained from running a successful national business, Nick implemented several small business start-ups and sold these business ventures along the way. Additionally he is the founder and current majority interest partner of Subtrack, a construction software development company.

Today Nick continues to work full time in the construction management field, he consults in the custom motorcycle industry building custom components and bikes, in addition to continuing to launch company start-ups and invest in real estate. In 1996 Nick also co-authored a college level text on Personal Finance.

978-0-595-47389

0-595-47389-X

CPSIA information can be obtained
at www.ICGtesting.com
Printed in the USA
FSHW011827110919
61932FS